Continuing the Journey

A Book for Parishes in Transition

Maureen Gallagher

Sheed & Ward

Sheed & Ward™ is a service of National Catholic Reporter Publishing Company, Inc.

Library of Congress Catalog Card Number: 88-62607

ISBN: 1-55612-238-1

Published by: Sheed & Ward
                115 E. Armour Blvd. P.O. Box 419492
                Kansas City, MO 64141-6492

To order, call: (800) 333-7373

Contents

Introduction

This book is designed to be used by groups of people in parishes who are experiencing changes which significantly affect parish life. In some cases the transitions will include moving from having a resident priest to having a parish life coordinator. At other times it may be the change of having one pastor per parish to sharing one pastor among several parishes or the move from each parish having its own religious education program or school to having interparish collaborative or consolidated programs. No matter what the change, if it is of a significant nature, parishes are faced with great loss.

The chapters in this book deal with stages many groups go through as they move through the process of grieving the loss of something important to the life of the community. While there are certain commonalities in the grieving process not all groups experience grief in the same way or over the same period of time. Grief cannot be programmed over a period of six weeks or six months or six years because so many circumstances affect the process. Keeping this in mind it is important when using this book to be sensitive to where the group is in the grieving process. Rushing through chapters to keep a predetermined timeline can be counterproductive. A group may wish to spend more time on one chapter than the leader had planned. Effective leaders are flexible and sensitive to group needs, allowing several sessions on one chapter if necessary.

The first chapter, "Remembering," invites groups to jog their memories and recall many events and various cultural elements from the past. It helps situate the current loss in the context of other changes the parish has experienced.

The second chapter, "Dealing with Loss," allows the groups to name their feelings and their experiences of loss. It paints a portrait of various feelings experienced during the grieving process from shock and dismay to anger and despair.

The third chapter, "Glimmers of Hope," begins to point to the light at the end of the tunnel. Despite the tragedy of loss, with all its miserable feelings, elements of hope are beginning to surface. These need to be nurtured.

The fourth chapter, "Working Through Problems," allows the group to name and deal with some of their pressing issues. It acknowledges that there are some things which are going better and attempts to focus the energies of the group.

The fifth chapter, "Envisioning the Future," empowers the group to build a new dream by imagining how things will be in a year or two. It channels the group's vitality and generates further momentum by challenging the group to create a new future structured around community worship and service.

The sixth chapter, "Creating a Ministering Community," focuses on the American Bishops' pastoral, "Called and Gifted." It suggests that the future will be lived out in the context of the laity realizing that they are called to adulthood, holiness, service and community. It is in responding to this call that people will experience the parishes of the 1990's.

This book is not a prize winning recipe to be followed with exactitude. It is a resource which is designed to help parish groups name and act upon their experiences of loss. The more it is seen as a resource and adapted to local circumstances, the more valuable it will be to parish groups. Not all exercises need to be used nor do all questions need to be answered.

I wish to express my gratitude to the many participants who shared their parish transitions at the symposium held at the Institute for Pastoral Life in Kansas City, Missouri, November, 1987. I also express deep appreciation to J. Gordon Myers, S.J., whose research on group life has allowed me to name in a certain logical framework the grieving process inherent in these pages.

I.

Remembering

Memories are very powerful. They put us in contact with the past by making it come alive. Memories evoke emotion. Recalling childhood Christmas traditions often stirs up feelings of warmth and joy. Remembering a loved one who has died conjures up sad memories. Remembrances can motivate people to greatness. When a person brings to mind words about striving for excellence of a favorite parent, teacher or coach, the person may get that extra push to keep on going despite obstacles. Sometimes memories are in need of healing. Tragic relationships or events can exert a negative influence many years after the event or relationship occurred. These memories can often be healed through prayer, therapy, and supportive friends.

The Judeo-Christian tradition places extraordinary value on memory. The Passover is a celebration which has been ritualized for over three thousand years. It memorializes God's saving action with the Jewish people. In this context Jesus, too, asked his friends to remember him when they came together to praise God, to recall God's action and to share a meal. We keep Jesus' memory alive at the Eucharist.

At times of transition and loss it is helpful to recall our roots. It is advantageous to be able to talk about from where we have come. Spending some time on this process allows

1

us to reflect upon the good times, the hard times, the moments of struggle as well as the great times.

Exercise 1
From Where Did We Come?

   a. Think about where you came from when you joined
       the parish. Circle the direction on the diagram. If you
       always lived in the parish, go back to your parents or
       grandparents, from where did they come to join the
       parish. Recall what you know about your early roots
       in the parish.

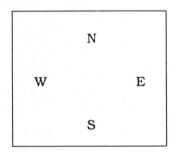

   b. What circumstances brought you to the parish?

c. What was your initial experience of the parish?

d. What priests, sisters, catechists do you remember fondly?

e. What deceased parishioners do you remember who contributed to the parish's spirit?

f. What memories do you share as a group?

g. What characteristics describe these group memories? (lifegiving, tragic, humorous, etc.)

A. Storytelling

Storytelling is a very important activity. It not only helps us remember but it helps us interpret our past and gives us our present identity. Stories put us in touch with another's world, invite us to live in that world for a few moments with all its trials and tribulations. Finally and almost magically, good stories help us return to our own world with new appreciations.

At a time of transition and loss, storytelling and listening to stories from the past are very important. It is not unusual after the funeral of a loved one for a family to sit around and share photographs, old movies, videos and stories of the deceased. Stories link us to the past while at the same time they give us a framework for meaning in the present and motivate us for the future.

Listening to stories about the parish from the past helps us to see the present from a certain perspective. We begin to see the change we are expected to cope with on a continuum of other changes the parish has experienced. Stories also help us to focus on what is really important about who we are as a parish.

When we listen to stories we become aware that these stories even to be remembered must have had an impact on the storyteller. To grasp the importance of the story we need to look at what convictions are inherent in the story. In other words, what are the underlying assumptions about the work of the parish. Lastly, as we listen to or tell stories we can see and name the moral sensitivities imbedded in the account. Did they point to a pastor's concern for children, or a staff person's love for the elderly or the poor or the people's concern for the welfare of the pastor? What we need to grasp is the relational quality of the story.

One might hear stories like the following told by a seventy-eight year old husband and wife who had both lived in the same parish all their lives. Maria recalled a story about her first communion where the pastor visited each home after supper the night before first communion and brought old handkerchiefs for her mother to tie over their faucets so no one would forget and break their fasts. He reminded all to receive communion the next morning. Maria recalled the story and her dad's humorous remarks to the delight of all her listeners.

Her husband, Joseph, recalled the story about building the church. He noted how every Saturday the men would gather to help with the building. He told of how once the roof was on the church the pastor slept on the floor of the new building so he wouldn't have to travel twenty miles back and forth to town on horseback to offer Mass on Sunday. When Joe's mother heard about that, she made Joe sleep on the floor in their kitchen so Father could have his bed.

Certain values surface in these stories. These values give the community its identity. One sees a) a pastor who knows his people, who visits homes, who appreciates the Eucharist and wants entire families to celebrate it together; b) the humor of the pastor and family; c) a community who works together; d) a priest who copes with primitive living conditions in order to serve; d) a family who opens its home and extends hospitality.

Exercise 2

a. Recall or listen to stories about your parish (i.e. pastor, missions, building programs, etc.). What do these stories tell you about your past?

b. What values do you find in the stories?

c. What do they tell you about your present identity?

d. Name values based on stories of the past that you want to maintain in the future.

e. As a group, what kind of stories have you recalled? What impact have these stories had on you as a group?

f. From your knowledge of the history of your parish what do you consider to be the four most important events up until this point in history? Write a few words or draw a symbol of these in the space below.

   1.

   2.

   3.

   4.

g.   Why do you think these events are most significant?

What kind of change was involved in each event?

How did you experience God's presence in these changes?

B. Remembering Our Culture

In the past there were many expressions of who we were. The statues in our churches reminded us of patron saints and beloved heroes and heroines.   Decorations helped us focus on seasonal events. Vestments and altar vessels set a tone or mood for a liturgical celebration.   Black vestments immediately told us we were remembering a deceased person.   Solemn High Masses indicated a great feast or event. The placement of the altar and pulpit all pointed out the things which the Church found most significant at a particular point in time.

Guadalupe celebrations, May crownings, St. Patrick's and St. Joseph Day festivities along with "Sorrowful Mother" or "Our Lady of Perpetual Help" novenas all were and in some parishes continue to be indicators of the culture in parish life.

Music is another very important element in our culture. Music helps form communities and gives them a sense of identity.   In the past, many parishes were familiar with Latin hymns (O Salutaris) and Marian hymns (O Mary We Crown Thee...) and moving marches (An Army of Youth). This music gave us an identity and a spirituality. It helped us "feel" Catholic.

Exercise 3

a. Recall some of the cultural expressions of the parish in the past.

b. Were there statues in church that are no longer there? What were they? Why were they important?

c. Do you have memories of certain seasonal decorations? Describe them.

d. What festivities or devotional practices do you recall?

e. The oldest songs or hymns you remember singing in this Church are:

f. Religious songs you remember from your high school days are:

g. What images of God, Jesus, Mary were present in your favorite songs or hymns?

Remembering situates us on life's journey and helps us see change as part of the journey. Remembering helps us deal with loss without losing what is essential to the present and the future.

Prayer and Ritual

Gathering Song "Gather Us In" (Verses 1 & 2), by Marty Haugen or a favorite song named in previous discussions.

Call To Prayer

Leader: God of the universe, you have called us to
be your people. You have stayed with us
and supported us throughout the ages.
We have heard many stories of your
presence amongst us. Now in this time of
change make your presence known to us
again as we recall your help in the past.

We ask this through Jesus, our Lord and friend. AMEN.

Reading   In one of the ancient stories of our tradition we are called to remember what God has done for us.

Exodus 13:3-5

Moses said to the people, "Keep this day in remembrance, the day you came out of Egypt, from the house of slavery, for it was by sheer power that Yahweh brought you out of it; no leavened bread must be eaten. On this day, in the month of Abib, you are leaving Egypt.

Reflection   What is the connection between this ancient story and the other stories we have heard at this gathering?

Response   Psalm 65:9-13 (adapted)

Men: You visit the earth and water it,
  you load it with riches;
God's rivers brim with water
  to provide their grain.

Women: This is how you provide it:
by drenching its furrows, by levelling
its ridges,
by softening it with showers, by blessing
the first fruits.

All: You crown the year with your bounty,
abundance flows wherever you pass;
the desert pastures overflow;
the hillsides are wrapped in joy,
the meadows are dressed in flocks,

the valleys are clothed in wheat,
what shouts of joy, what singing!

Ritualizing Our Memories

Leader: God, creator of us all, we have come to this
            parish from the North, South, East and West
            to be your people, to worship you as our God
            and to be your presence for one another.

Presentation of Water from North, South, East and West

Person representing the North:

We have come from the North, from ____ ____ ____
(name specific places) in search of your presence which we
found at (name of parish) _____. Continue to be with
us in our lives, in our struggles and in our prayer.

Person representing the South:

We have come from the opposite direction, the South. We
have come over many years from places like ____ ____ ____
(name specific places) to worship in your house and carry
your Word with us. Continue to entrust us with your word
as we take it into our lives.

Person representing the East:

We have come from the East, the land of the morning sun.
We have seen your sun rise in ____ ____ ____ (name
specific places), before we came here. We have experienced
the light of your life in all of our lives as we try to reflect your
values and bring your new light of morning to our days.

Person representing the West:

We have come from the West, the land of your setting sun. We have come from ____ ____ ____ (name specific places), with confidence that you are with us even in darkness. Stay with us as we continue to grow in our understanding of your justice and mercy in our lives.

Blessing of Water

Leader: Recognizing God's presence in our past as well as God's presence with us now,

All: We bless this water. It is the water of our lives and our efforts to bring a renewed appreciation for God's presence. May God continue to shower blessings on us in the name of Jesus. AMEN.

Leader: (Bless all with water using a small branch from a bush or tree)

Concluding Prayer

Leader: God, we have come here to recall your presence among us over the years. We have taken time to see how even through many changes you have continued to be with us. We believe that now in our time of transition, you continue to support us and be with us. We ask your help to continue to support us in the name of Jesus.

All: AMEN.

Closing Song "We Are Many Parts" by Marty Haugen or other appropriate song.

II.

Dealing with Loss

Anytime a parish undergoes change, no matter how positive or negative the change might be, there are always elements of loss. When a parish loses a school or when a parish religious education program becomes an interparish collaborative program loss is experienced. The consolidation of parishes brings with it a significant sense of loss of parish identity and parish tradition. When a parish loses its resident priest pastor the whole community experiences loss. Not only is there the loss of a person who may have been beloved by the parishioners, but there is an even deeper loss. An underlying assumption can no longer be held.

Most contemporary American Catholics grew up with the assumption that they would always have a local parish and that their parish would always be provided with a priest. Some people experienced being part of what was often called a "mission parish." While they were not a self-sufficient parish they always had their own identity and shared a priest with one or two other parishes.

American Catholics were used to pastors being changed over their lifetime. They realized bishops made clergy assignments. Many had their favorite pastors but most never questioned whether they would have a pastor or not. Sometimes they did not get pastors they particularly liked but they always had a priest. Based on their experience many assumed it was their God-given right. Consequently, not having a resident pastor can be a profound change for a parish. This chapter deals with the various stages of coping with loss. While the cause of the loss may vary, the stages of dealing with it are rather consistent. They include: (1) shock and disbelief; (2) anger and protest; and (3) depression and despair.

A. Shock and Disbelief

The following deals with one specific example. With the diminishing number of ordained clergy all parishes cannot have resident priests. When people experience this loss their reaction is one of shock. They wonder why this should happen to them. They may respond, "We have been good Catholics. We have contributed to the Church, why us?"

There is also a certain element of panic. "Where will we go to church?" "Who will take care of us?" "What will this mean? Will we lose our church too?"

When these things are talked about in formal or informal groups someone in the group will often say "Let's go to the bishop. I'm sure this is a mistake. He really didn't mean what he said. He must be able to get more priests from somewhere."

The shock, the panic and denial are often people's first response to loss. This is especially true if the experience of loss has been sudden. The more preparation there can be for the change the less severe are the responses to it.

Exercise 1

Put a check in front of the sentences to which you can relate in some way.

1. ___ The bishop's just kidding. He wants us to work harder at being good Catholics and contribute more to the diocese.

2. ___ The diocesan planners didn't get all the data. Wait till they get the facts from us.

3. ___ The bishop doesn't know enough about us. Once he knows who we really are, he'll see things differently.

4. ___ I'm sure he'll change his mind when he meets with us.

5. ___ Let's just continue with our parish council plans for the coming year. Maybe it will all go away.

6. ___ Let's just get on with it. It's no big deal.

7. ___ Bishops never did treat us fairly.

8. ___ Why isn't (*Parish Name*) doing without a priest?

9. ___ I'm going to go to another Church.

10. ___ Others (write yours)

Exercise 2   How Did I Feel When...

a. Think about your feelings when you first heard that you would be or might be losing a resident priest.

b. What image or words best describe your feelings?

c. Why do you think you felt this way?

d. What words describe your feelings as a group who first discovered the situation?

B. Anger and Protest

As people get more accustomed to the fact that there will be changes at their parish they react differently. Some may welcome it for various theological or personal reasons. But many will be angry and protest the decision. They yearn for the past. They may blame the parish council for not being strong enough. They may blame the pastor or former pastors for not being an effective advocate with the bishop. Anger needs a target. During times of organizational change anger is often misplaced and lands on the nearest visible target. Eventually people may blame themselves. "We were too hard on our priests." A less obvious expression of loss is the glorification of the past. As people talk about the loss of their resident pastor they may exaggerate how wonderful everything has been, remembering none of the problems or hardships. They simply want things to be as they once were in the "good ole days." They romanticize all that has been through rose colored glasses.

Exercise 3

    a.   Name some of the benefits you as a group experienced by having a resident pastor.

1. _____   6. _____

2. _____   7. _____

3. _____   8. _____

4. _____   9. _____

5. _____   10. _____

    b.   Which of these benefits do you as a group feel will no longer be available to you?

    c.   How do you as a group feel about these losses?

C. Depression and Despair

A later stage in the response to loss is despair.

Sometimes when people take the loss of a resident pastor very hard they become depressed. They feel very abandoned—even deserted by God. A cloud of doom hangs over the parish. At other times the experience of deprivation brings forth feelings of apathy. People who were once active in the parish walk away from involvement. There's a "what's the use" attitude. One will hear, "We've tried but the bishop (or the diocesan planner) won't change his mind. Now everyone is doing his or her own thing. Nothing hangs together."

The "let's give up" attitude reflects exhaustion, a feeling that everything is near collapse. The earlier sense of panic which sparked energy has given way to boredom. Any unexpressed anger is reflected in involvement in other aspects of life to replace the efforts toward building up the parish or even participating in parish life. Here people stop struggling with the inevitable. They live with "it's all over; we won't have a resident pastor ever." At this point some people will "take a long vacation from the church."

Exercise 4

a. Think of times when you experienced loss in the past. (Loss of a loved one, friend, home, pet, job, car, etc.) How is the loss of a resident pastor similar? Different?

b.   In what way did you deal similarly with the loss? Differently?

c.   As a group, what images surface if your feelings are close to despair? (Example: Ship without a rudder, tribe without a chief, etc.)

Prayer and Ritual

Opening Song   "Bless the Lord" or another appropriate song

Call To Prayer

Leader: God, beholder of us all, you have given us your presence in your church and in your world. Help us to recognize your presence in the lives of those who have preceded us in this parish. Enable us to recognize that same presence in our lives today. We ask this in the name of Jesus.

All: AMEN.

Introduction to the Reading:

It is good to reflect in times of loss on what is essential to our lives—our faith. That is not unique to us. Many who have gone before us shared the same faith. How we live out our faith changes from era to era, but the gift from

God is the same for all generations. As we are in the midst of upheaval it is helpful to take time to appreciate anew our gift of faith. Our parishes are built upon faith. Our parish communities are designed to help us make faith a living reality. How parishes do this changes, but faith is steadfast. As a group we are nourished by faith.

Reading

2 Timothy, 1-7

From Paul, appointed by God to be an apostle of Christ Jesus in the design to promise life in Christ Jesus; to Timothy, dear child of mine, wishing you grace, mercy and peace from God the Creator and from Christ Jesus our Lord.

Night and day I thank God, keeping my conscience clear and remembering my duty to the Lord as my ancestors did, and always I remember you in my prayers; I remember your tears and long to see you again to complete my happiness. Then I am reminded of the sincere faith which you have; it came first to live in your grandmother Lois, and your mother Eunice, and I have no doubt that is the same faith in you as well.

That is why I am reminding you now to fan into a flame the gift that God gave you when I laid my hands on you. God's gift was not a spirit of timidity, but the Spirit of power, and love, and self-control.

Reflection

General Intercession from the Community. Response: Lord, Hear Our Prayer.

Ritual Of Light	Eight designated people individually light a candle after the community says: "Lord, enlighten our way."
Leader:	Jesus, giver of all good things we stand with confidence during these times of transition as we ask for gifts to help us on our way, (silent prayer)
All:	Lord, Enlighten Our Way
Leader:	For the gift of flexibility to work with others in times of uncertainty, (silent prayer)
All:	Lord, Enlighten Our Way
Leader:	For the gift of understanding to stand in the shoes of the other to truly "stand under" our brothers and sisters, (silent prayer)
All:	Lord, Enlighten Our Way
Leader:	For the gift of poverty to let go of those things that are not essential to you to rid our lives of all that does not matter, (silent prayer)
All:	Lord, Enlighten Our Way
Leader:	For the gift of endurance for energy to keep going despite discouragement and to believe that you are present in the upheaval, (silent prayer)

All:	Lord, Enlighten Our Way
Leader:	For the gift of expectation to stand on tiptoe with all of creation to wait for rebirth, for the new advent, (silent prayer)
All:	Lord, Enlighten Our Way
Leader:	For the gift of reverence to be gentle with the mystery of each other's uniqueness to stand on holy ground and acknowledge the value of creation, (silent prayer)
All:	Lord, Enlighten Our Way
Leader:	We pray in gratitude for all that has been given us. We try to make your reign more visible on earth. (silent prayer)
All:	Lord, Enlighten Our Way
Closing Song	"Prayer of St. Francis" by Sebastian Temple or another appropriate song

III.

Glimmers of Hope

Over time and after many opportunities for expression the sad and angry feelings associated with major parish changes begin to diminish. From the shock, anger and despair hope of new life begins to emerge. Gradually there is acceptance of the fact that a parish will no longer have a resident pastor.

In one sense the crisis brought about has been an experience of death for the parish. Something important which was always there is gone. Not only is a person gone but a faithfully held assumption is also gone. No longer will things be the same. This shock to the parish has elicited many elements of grief. Rooted deeply in the Christian tradition is the belief that there is life after death—that good things can come from bad.

On Holy Saturday we proclaim "Oh Happy Fault"—from human inadequacy, incompleteness and sin has come new life, redemption and resurrection. Jesus often spoke of the "new life" amidst the darkness and chaos. He told of the grain of wheat which needed to die before it could sprout forth new life. He spoke of the vine which needed pruning before it could produce a healthy harvest. Deep within our heritage is belief in the death-resurrection mystery of Jesus' life as well as our own lives.

Exercise 1

a. From your own experience name some wonderful things which can only come about after something has died or been cut away.

b. Describe how the new life comes about.

c. How does this relate to the death-resurrection mystery Jesus spoke about and lived?

d. What is your favorite image of new life? Why?

e. As a group decide what words you would use to describe new life.

A. Signs of New Life

It is difficult at times of profound change to see anything positive, to see any light at the end of the tunnel. The sense of loss overwhelms us and closes in on us. But gradually after our loss is acknowledged hope emerges.

At first it is like the new shoot of a spring plant. Amidst the debris of the dead autumn remnants a tiny yellowish stem shows its tip. It's vulnerable. A hard frost could kill it. A heavy rake could cut it off at the ground. Too much water could rot it. Too little could dehydrate it.

Hope expressed in a group experiencing profound change is much like a new fragile sprout. When a few positive results of the change begin to emerge they may be cut down by those who continue to mourn the past. They may be misunderstood by those who need to be stuck in denial or despair for a while more. They may die from lack of nourishment from those who are too insecure to embrace new ideas.

Eventually, however, the energy for new life overcomes the resistance and the change is viewed as at least workable, if not fully embraced.

Exercise 2

Recall some of the previous changes you have had to make in your life. List both the losses and the positive things which came from the loss. Note how you feel about the event now.

Example

Change: I lost my job due to a corporate takeover, or I
           lost my job because the farm was sold to a big
           corporation.

	Losses	Gains
Income, Security		It forced me to get trained for new work. Now I have a better job.

Present Feelings: "Best thing that ever happened to me."

Change:

Losses	Gains

Present Feelings:

Exercise 3

Recall previous changes at your parish. List both the losses and the gains and your present feelings about the changes.

a. Change:

Losses   Gains

Present Feelings:

b. What common experiences or outlooks do you have with others in your group?

Exercise 4

As you examine the change or expected change currently in your parish, name some of the losses and the gains as well as your current feelings.

a. Change:

Losses   Gains

Present Feelings:

b.   As a group, how would you describe your current
        reaction to the change in your parish?

B. Signs of Hope in the Parish

As people begin to see that some good things can come out
of loss they begin to consider committing themselves to help
create a renewed parish.   Optimism gradually overcomes
hopeless feelings.   One begins to hear such comments as,
"Well, maybe we can now get more involved in the parish."
"A consolidated school is better than no school." "Yeah, I
have a few ideas about the youth program." "Maybe our
parish could become a model for the diocese!" "Now I bet we'll
only see the people who really want to make something out of
this."

Exercise 5

a. Write some of the positive comments you have heard lately in your parish.

b. As a group, what is the most positive thing you can say about the current situation?

Exercise 6

a. What image comes to your mind as you see a few rays of hope in your community?
(Example: It's like the first shoots of a spring flower...or, it's like a few rays of sun on a mostly cloudy day...)
Name or draw your image.

b. Decide on an image which best fits your group now.

Prayer And Ritual

Gathering Song "On Eagle's Wings," by Michael Joncas, or another appropriate song

Call To Prayer

Leader: God, giver of hope, help us to see the elements of new life which are interwoven with the elements of loss. Enable us to begin to pull together and to design what will be our future. We ask this in the name of Jesus.

All: AMEN.

Introduction To The Reading:

Just as the disciples on the road to Emmaus were dealing with loss, so are we. Just as they began to find meaning in what had taken place in the previous days, so are we. Let us listen to their story which is becoming our story.

Reading Luke 24, 13-32

That very same day, two of them were on their way to a village called Emmaus, seven miles from Jerusalem, and they were talking together about all that had happened. Now as they talked this over, Jesus himself came up and walked by their side; but something prevented them from recognizing him. He said to them, "What matters are you discussing as you walk along?" They stopped short, their faces downcast.

Then one of them, called Cleopas, answered him, "You must be the only person staying

in Jerusalem who does not know the things
that have been happening there these days."
"What things?" he asked. "All about Jesus of
Nazareth," they answered, "who proved he
was a great prophet by the things he said
and did in the sight of God and of the whole
people; and how our chief priests and our
leaders handed him over to be sentenced to
death, and had him crucified. Our own hope
had been that he would be the one to set
Israel free. And this is not all: two whole days
have gone by since it all happened; and some
women from our group have astounded us:
they went to the tomb in the early morning,
and when they did not find the body, they
came back to tell us they had seen a vision
of angels who declared he was alive. Some of
our friends went to the tomb and found
everything exactly as the women had reported,
but of him they saw nothing."

When they drew near to the village to which
they were going, he made as if to go on; but
they pressed him to stay with them. "It is
nearly evening" they said "and the day is
almost over." So he went in to stay with
them. Now while he was with them at table,
he took the bread and said the blessing; then
he broke it and handed it to them. And their
eyes were opened and they recognized him;
but he had vanished from their sight.

Reflection   What do we have in common with the disciples
on the road to Emmaus?

Ritualizing Our Hopes

The Weaver: A Community Story

Leader: For many years...for many, many years...
           Martha had been the town weaver. She
           wove a very special scarf. The scarf protected
           the people from the snow, sand, cold and
           the bitterness of winter. All the people
           recognized this long scarf. When people
           wore the scarf others remarked about its
           great quality. It was truly outstanding.
           The whole town was involved in some way or
           other in helping the weaver. Some cooked
           her meals. Some cleaned her house. Some
           watched her children so she could continue
           to weave the scarves that kept people warm.

           A great crisis came to the town. Martha was
           running out of the special kind of yarn
           needed for her garment. The deep purple
           color could not be found. How would the
           people keep warm?

All: HOW WILL WE KEEP WARM?

Leader: The dye makers had changed their colors.
           Deep purple was becoming very scarce. Of
           late only about half the strands of deep
           purple were found in every scarf. The people
           thought it was this very deep color which
           kept them warm. Now, how would the
           people keep warm?

All: HOW WILL WE KEEP WARM?

Leader: People kept coming to Martha and begging
           her to save some of her very special deep

purple yarn for them. She started splitting
the strands of yarn. The deep purple was
getting thinner and thinner. Martha started
twisting the deep purple with other colors so
it would be stronger and not break as she
wove it into the scarves that kept people
warm. Gradually, Martha could do no more.
She still was a wonderful weaver, but she
only had one last skein of deep purple yarn.
She called to the villagers,

Voice 1: Bring your yarn and I will weave warm
scarves with your yarn.

But they didn't believe their yarn would work.
It wasn't the special deep purple. How
would the people keep warm?

All: HOW WILL WE KEEP WARM?

Leader: She called again,

Voice 1: Bring your yarn.

Leader: No one came.

Martha was a very wise woman. She knew
the villagers' yarn was good. She knew it
was strong. She knew it would keep them
warm. The wise Martha also knew she
needed the people to look at their yarn again.
To see it with new eyes.

She called out one more time.

Voice 1: Go to your closets. Go to the bottom of your
baskets. Select your best yarn. Take your
yarn in your hands. Twist it. Pull it. Coddle

	it. This is the thread of your life. Tell me of your yarn.
Leader:	One old woman brought Martha some precious yarn and said,
Voice 2:	This is yarn my mother gave me. I've saved it for many years. Once I made a sweater for my daughter with it. After she died at an early age, I took the sweater and unwove it, to save the yarn for another child. Another child never came. I give you my yarn to weave into a warm scarf for someone else.
Voice 1:	Thank you for your yarn. Thank you for your life.
Leader:	Once again the weaver called out,
Voice 1:	Tell me of your yarn. Tell me of your life.
Leader:	All were quiet. Then a young couple came forth.
Voices 3-4:	Here is our yarn. It is new yarn. We cannot give you separate yarn. Our yarn is interwoven. Our strength is in our togetherness. Take our yarn. Weave it into a warm scarf.
Voice 1:	Thank you for your yarn. Thank you for your life.
Leader:	The weaver repeated her call,
Voice 1:	Tell me of your yarn, tell me of your life.
Leader:	After a long pause a strong man came forward. His yarn was the coarse threads of a potato sack.

Voice 5:	Take my yarn. It is not colorful. But it is strong. It can carry food to people. With softer yarn it can keep people warm.
Voice 1:	Thank you for your yarn. Thank you for your life.
Leader:	Once again the woman called out.
Voice 1:	Tell me of your yarn. Tell me of your life.
Leader:	She called out one more time.
Voice 1:	Go to your closets. Go to the bottom of your baskets, select your best yarn. Take your yarn in your hands. Twist it. Pull it. Coddle it. This is the thread of your life. Tell me of your yarn. (Individuals invited to share yarn and the meaning of the yarn.)
Leader:	And the people began to take their yarn to the weaver.
All:	(After each presentation of yarn, respond) "THANK YOU FOR YOUR YARN. THANK YOU FOR YOUR LIFE."
Ending:	The weaver continued to weave. People continued to bring their yarn. Her deep purple yarn went further than anyone ever expected. The weaver showed others how to weave. They often wove small scarves which she connected with other scarves. The scarves looked different than they had many years ago. But the weaver made them strong and warm. People soon learned to love the scarves of many colors.
All:	Sing an Alleluia or other appropriate song.

IV.

Working Through Problems

As new life begins to emerge in a group, the group surfaces some energy to begin to deal with problems. For instance, after a group comes to accept the fact over time that they can no longer maintain a parish Catholic school, they may seek alternatives in consolidated schools or ask a certain parish to run a primary grade school and another to administrate an intermediate grade school. Or a parish who has lost its church through a tragic fire may begin to nurture its glimmers of hope by forming a new building committee to contact architects.

Beginning to cope with the future is a sign that new life is taking hold. The parish which is told that it will have a parish life coordinator instead of a resident pastor at first may suffer shock and dismay. Later despair and depression may overtake the group. Eventually new sparks of life emerge and people begin to ask questions like who will hire the parish life coordinator? What will the job be? When will the person begin? These questions may be answered very differently from diocese to diocese or parish to parish. Some diocesan offices hire parish life coordinators according to a fixed job description. Others create the job description with the parish and involve the parish in the hiring process. No matter what role the diocese and the parish assume in the transition process, certain tasks need to be accomplished. Problem solving is a framework used to come to decisions about what needs to be done. Many of the transition decisions and tasks can be expedited through a problem solving process. For instance, in the move from a resident pastor to a parish life coordinator, many questions will need to be answered and problems will need to be solved. Relationship issues like the role of the parish life coordinator and the relationship of the coordinator to the parish council, sacramental minister, etc. need to be addressed.

The process of addressing these and other problems suggested here involves six steps:

1. identifying the problem;

2. generating alternative solutions;

3. evaluating alternative solutions;

4. deciding the best workable solution;

5. implementing the solution, and

6. evaluating the solution.

Note that the overall term "problem solving" is being used here in its broadest sense to include decision making and the naming and accomplishment of tasks. A group does not need a "big problem" or "major conflict" to find the problem solving framework helpful.

A. Identifying the Problem

The first step in the process is to define what the problem is. This step calls for clear thinking and the ability to isolate one thing from another. For instance, how to bring about a smooth transition—from a resident priest to a parish life coordinator, or from individual parish schools to a consolidated school system—are stated too generally. They need to be broken down into manageable parts such as: how to present the parish life coordinator to the parish or how to involve the parish council in the selection of the parish life coordinator or school principal. The problem statement should be very clear and include the desired outcome, i.e., presentation of parish life coordinator to parish or selection of the parish administrator.

Exercise 1

    a.   As a group names problems to be solved, decisions to be made or tasks to be accomplished relative to the transition your parish is making.

Examples:

- How to set up a parish council interview committee

- How to plan a "Meet the Parish Life Coordinator" evening

- How to enable the religious education committee to set goals

- How to develop staff job descriptions

- How to enable the liturgy committee to design alternatives for community prayer

- How to involve joint school boards in developing a single school philosophy

- How will the parish life coordinator relate to the sacramental minister

- How will the parish understand the role of the parish life coordinator

- How to write a job description for the parish life coordinator

Problems or tasks our group is dealing with include:

1.

2.

3.

4.

5.

Reexamine the problems to be sure that they are stated clearly and that not more than one problem is stated in each instance.

B. Looking for Solutions

The second step in problem solving is to brainstorm solutions. It is important at this step to generate as many possible solutions as can be imagined. No evaluation happens at this stage. One way to do this is to ask each individual in the group to take some quiet time and write all imaginable solutions to the problem without considering if the solutions are adequate for the problem or not. After the individuals have done this, all can share one solution at a time while attempting to avoid sharing duplicate suggestions. The process will generate many solutions.

For instance, if the problem was "How to initiate the parish life coordinator into parish life" some of the brainstormed solutions might include:

a) introduce the person at all the weekend Masses

b) have a parish pot luck to introduce the person

c) have the person intern with Father Smith for a month

d) have the person meet with the parish council

e) have the person meet with all the parish committees

f) have the person chair the parish festival committee

g) have the bishop come and introduce the parish life coordinator

h) have the person talk at all the Masses

i) have the person visit all the homes in the parish

j) have area "coffees" to welcome the parish life coordinator

k) have coffee and donuts after all the Masses to meet the parish life coordinator

l) have the parish council understand the parish life coordinator job description and discuss mutual expectations. (See samples of parish life coordinators' job descriptions at the end of this chapter. If you need to write one keep in mind the need to have clear elements of accountability. Diocesan offices can be very helpful in this regard. This assumes the diocese hired the parish life coordinator and provided the job description. This is not always the process favored.)

Exercise 2

a. Choose one problem from exercise one. Brainstorm all possible solutions to the problem defined above. Remember, do not evaluate them at this time.

1.

2.

3.

4.

5.

6.

7.

8.

9.

10.

b. In a "round robin" share one solution at a time until all have shared their list of solutions. If one of your solutions is similar to someone else's and is already on the list, go on to your next solution.

c. Ask for clarity if need be, but do not discuss solutions at this point.

C. Evaluating Solutions

At this step in the process each solution is evaluated in terms of its appropriateness. Some solutions will be eliminated as impossible or not desired. As an example, examine the solutions generated in the sample exercise above. Note the kind of critical thinking that is demanded at this point. This is done most effectively individually first and then shared through group discussion.

a. Introduce the person at all the Masses.
Thinking:
This would be good exposure for the parish life coordinator, but more is needed.

b. Have a parish pot luck to introduce the person.
Thinking:
This might work but many people probably wouldn't be able to come because they'll be in the fields this time of year or most parish pot lucks mainly attract older women so only a small number of parishioners would be included.

c. Have the person intern with Father Smith.
Thinking:
This is impossible because the person cannot start until May 15 and Father Smith will be gone on May 1. So this solution needs to be eliminated.

d. Have the person meet with the parish council.
Thinking:
This is a good idea, but more orientation is needed.

e. Have the person meet with all parish committees.
Thinking:
This is another good idea, but more exposure is needed.

f. Have the person chair the festival committee.
Thinking:
This is not a good idea, person needs to know the parish before chairing this committee. Eliminate this solution.

The kind of thinking needed at this evaluation step is evident from the above examples. The end result of this step is to come to a list of desirable solutions.

Exercise 3

a. Evaluate brainstormed solutions using critical thinking skills for your own problem.

1.

2.

3.

4.

5.

6.

7.

8.

9.

10.

b.   Name the eliminated solutions.

c.   Name the solutions or combination of solutions
which you now consider real possibilities.

D. Deciding the Best Workable Solution

The fourth step in problem solving is to make a decision on the best solution to the problem.   Often this may be a combination of several of the possible solutions named in the previous steps.

The ideal is to have the solution backed by the consensus of the group.   In the above example the final solution might be something like this:

To initiate the new parish life coordinator the parish will:

a.   have the person meet the parish council and the
committees

b.   have the bishop come and introduce the person at
all the Masses

c.   have area "coffees" to welcome the parish life
coordinator

d.   have coffee and donuts after all the Masses in June
to welcome the person

e.   have the parish council understand the parish life
coordinator's job description and discuss mutual
expectations.

Exercise 4

Decide on the solution to be implemented for your own problem.

E. Implementing the Solution

Now that the solution has been decided upon, steps need to be developed to implement it. One way to do this is to decide who will do what and by when will the task be completed. In order to do that activities need to be distributed, priorities set and timelines developed.

In the above example, some of the steps in implementation might include the following:

a. Decide the order in which things needs to be accomplished.

  • Contact the Bishop
  • Schedule parish council and committee meetings
  • Schedule "coffees"

b. Get volunteers to do specific tasks.
  • Mary will write to the Bishop
  • Juan will schedule parish council meetings
  • Leanora will get volunteers to provide "coffees"

c. Build in timelines

  • Mary will write the Bishop by April 15
  • Juan will schedule meetings by May 1

- Leanora will get volunteers to provide "coffees" by May 1

d.   Implement the plans

Exercise 5

Outline some plans for the implementation of the solution in Exercise 4.   Use the example above to help focus your plans.

F. Evaluation

The solution of a problem solved needs to be evaluated. One way to evaluate the solution to a problem is to: 1) develop criteria for the evaluation; 2) look for evidence to support or negate the criteria, and 3) form a judgement by comparing the criteria and the evidence.

An example of this step in the problem solved above might include the following:

Criteria

- The new parish life coordinator feels welcome.

- People in the parish recognize the name and face of the parish life coordinator.

- The parish councils understands the role of the parish life coordinator.

- The parish life coordinator understands the expectations of the parish council.

Evidence

• Several weeks after the implementation, the parish life coordinator was interviewed to assess feelings about the introduction to the parish. The parish life coordinator felt very welcomed and enjoyed working in the parish.

• Many people greet the parish life coordinator by name after Sunday Mass.

• The parish council passed a resolution of support for the new parish life coordinator.

• The parish life coordinator has initiated several meetings with the parish council president to clarify roles. Both parties feel more work is needed in this area.

Judgement

Generally the solution to the problem of initiating the parish life coordinator to the parish achieved its goals. However, there is still some work needed on the clarity of roles.

Exercise 6

Returning to your problem solution and implementation plan, decide on the criteria needed to evaluate your solution. Make the criteria as specific as possible. Decide upon a reasonable timeline for your evaluation. Describe how the evidence will be gathered.

Method by which the evidence will be collected

Criteria   Target Date

1.

2.

3.

4.

5.

This chapter can be used and adapted to many situations. They basically help a group focus their energies on creating a preferred future. The process encourages groups to concentrate on what is possible and begin to build new life step by step. By breaking problems down into small manageable parts, a group which has been stressed by profound loss begins to mobilize its focus to plan for something better.

Prayer And Ritual

Gathering Song "Be Not Afraid," by John Foley, S.J., or another appropriate song

Call To Prayer

Leader: God, you have given us many resources to cope with the problems which we encounter in our lives. Empower us to help create a future where your presence can be known and manifest to all in our community. We ask you through your son and our brother, Jesus Christ.

All: AMEN.

Introduction to the Reading:

> Problems arise when people work together.
> The challenge of solving problems often leads
> to new insights and stretches people to come
> to new understandings and realizations. The
> early Church had its share of problems and
> misunderstandings to deal with. The following
> reading describes a problem that arose in the
> early Church and its solution.

Reading   Acts of the Apostles 15:1-12

> Then some men came down from Judaea and
> taught the brothers, "Unless you have
> yourselves circumcised in the tradition of
> Moses you cannot be saved." This led to
> disagreement, and after Paul and Barnabas
> had had a long argument with these men it
> was arranged that Paul and Barnabas and
> others of the church should go up to
> Jerusalem and discuss the problem with the
> apostles and elders.

> All the members of the church saw them off,
> and as they passed through Phoenicia and
> Samaria they told how the pagans had been
> converted and this news was received with
> the greatest satisfaction by the brothers.
> When they arrived in Jerusalem they were
> welcomed by the church and by the apostles
> and elders, and gave an account of all that
> God had done with them.

> But certain members of the Pharisees' party
> who had become believers objected, insisting

that the pagans should be circumcised and instructed to keep the Law of Moses. The apostles and elders met to look into the matter and after the discussion had gone on a long time, Peter stood up and addressed them.

My brothers, he said, you know perfectly well that in the early days God made his choice among you: the pagans were to learn the Good News from me and so become believers. In fact God, who can read everyone's heart, showed his approval of them by giving the Holy Spirit to them just as he had to us. God made no distinction between them and us, since he purified their hearts by faith. It would only provoke God's anger now, surely, if you imposed on the disciples the very burden that neither we nor our ancestors were strong enough to support? Remember, we believe that we are saved in the same way as they are: through the grace of the Lord Jesus.

This silenced the entire assembly, and they listened to Barnabas and Paul describing all the signs and wonders God had worked through them among the pagans.

For Reflection What are some things we have in common with the early Church?

Response Psalm 16 (adapted)

Men: Keep us, O God, for in you we take refuge;
How wonderfully has God made us cherish the holy ones who are in this land.

Women: We bless the Lord who counsels us;
even in the night our hearts exhort us.

We set the Lord ever before us,
with God at our right hand we shall
not be disturbed.

All:
Our hearts are glad and our souls rejoice;
Our bodies too abide in confidence;
You will not abandon us;
Nor will you suffer your faithful to
undergo corruption;
You will show us the path to life,
fullness of joys in your presence,
the delights at your right hand forever.

Ritualizing Our Leadership Abilities

Leader:
Problem solving is a leadership function of
the community. Recall the leadership qualities
you have exhibited in this transition time.
(Pause) God has given us leadership qualities
for the good of other people. The use of
these qualities reflects God's presence in the
community. Incense is a sign of God's
presence. It will be used in our prayer to
remind us of God's presence as we use our
leadership qualities to build our future together.

Prayer:
God, our leader and co-creator, we recognize
your presence in our struggles to solve the
problems we face in our daily lives. We
realize you have given us the opportunity to
come together and share our leadership abilities
to further your reign on earth. The mystery
of your presence both overwhelms and
supports us. We want you to continue to be
with us in both mystery and majesty.
We ask this in Jesus' name.

All:
AMEN.

Leader: (*Name individual or group*) I call you forward in the name of the community to acknowledge God's presence in your leadership.

If the parish life coordinator or other designated leaders are present, have them come forward individually to be incensed. After the individuals, have each small group come forward. As a sign of acknowledging God's presence have each person and group extend their arms and look to the heavens as they are incensed.

As each person and group comes forward and is incensed, the assembly prays: "...the Spirit of God has made us, the breath of the Almighty keeps us alive." Ps. 33: 4 (adapted)

After individuals and small groups have been incensed the prayer leader incenses the entire group.

Closing Prayer Assembled in a circle, pray the Lord's Prayer.

Closing Song "Holy God, We Praise Thy Name," or another appropriate song

Sample Job Description for Parish Life Coordinator

The appointment of a person other than a priest to be the official leader of a parish community involves the establishment of new ways of thinking and the development of new roles and relationships. In order that all parties concerned have as much clarity as possible about their rights and responsibilities when such an appointment is made, the following description is offered.

Parish Life Coordinator: any person, other than an ordained presbyter, who is appointed by the Bishop and is charged with the pastoral care of a parish or parishes.

Responsibilities

The Parish Life Coordinator has full responsibility for the pastoral care of a local parish community (with the exception of those areas which require the ministry of an ordained presbyter). This responsibility does not necessarily imply that the parish life coordinator is the person that actually performs all of the tasks involved in the life of the parish, but rather that much of that overall responsibility will be exercised through collaboration and delegation. Specifically, the responsibilities of the Parish Life Coordinator include:

a. Administration of the parish, including the making and keeping of budgets, all accounting responsibilities, preparation and keeping of all other necessary records and reports, and providing appropriate leadership and guidance for the parish finance council and the parish pastoral council (including presiding at meetings).

b. Religious formation of children, youth, and adults, including sacramental preparation and especially catechumenate.

c. Coordination and direction of liturgical celebration (in close cooperation with those who will provide priestly ministry).

d. Establishment and development of community, in such a way as to ensure community participation and provide for the development of local parish leaders.

e. Development within the parish of its communal sense of Christian mission for evangelization, outreach, and social action.

f. Ensuring clear and open communication between the parish and all diocesan structures and agencies.

g. Provisions for the involvement of the parish in ecumenical activities and the development of better ecumenical relations.

h. Exercising all of these responsibilities in a true spirit of collegiality and subsidiarity.

Job Description of Parish Life Coordinator

The Committee recommends the following job description with the expectation and assumption that the implementation of the various responsibilities outlined would be impossible for one person and would be appropriately delegated to other persons in the parish. A significant gift of leadership would be the ability to so delegate.

Accountability and Appointment:

The Parish Life Coordinator would:

• be assigned by the Archbishop to implement the vision and mission of the local Church;

• have appropriate responsibilities and authority delegated;

• be accountable directly to Vicar, ultimately to the Archbishop;

• meet quarterly or semi-annually with Vicar or his delegate;

• have an evaluation, as developed by the Personnel Department yearly by Vicar or his delegate, of ministry as Parish Life Coordinator;

• be responsible to develop and/or maintain Parish Mission Statement.

Proclamation and Teaching:

The Parish Life Coordinator would be responsible for seeing that the necessary personnel, structures and procedures are established:

• to proclaim the Good News to all through efforts in evangelization;

• to enable children, youth and adults to grow in their understanding and living of the Faith through life-long religious education and Catholic schooling, where appropriate;

• foster lay leaders in education and provide training, encouragement and enthusiasm for the proclaiming/teaching mission of the parish, especially the training and support of catechists;

• to see that the parish Education Committee receives appropriate assistance and direction.

Prayer and Worship:

The Parish Life Coordinator would be ultimately involved in the prayer life of the community:

The Parish Life Coordinator would be responsible for:

• arranging for the regular celebration of the Eucharist;

• seeing that the Sacraments are administered—Baptism, Confirmation, Marriage, Anointing, Eucharist, Reconciliation, funerals. Adequate preparation program should be provided in reaching out to the sick and shut-ins with prayer and Sacrament;

• maintaining communication with and supporting the Sacramental Minister;

• including the Sacramental Minister in community life where appropriate;

• seeing that people receive assistance in developing their own personal prayer lives;

• Recruiting and training or providing training for liturgical ministers, lectors, cantors, ministers of the Eucharist, musicians, etc.;

• to see to the coordination of preparation and planning for the major feasts and seasons, especially Advent/Christmas, Lent/Holy Week/Easter;

• to see that the parish Liturgy Committee receives appropriate assistance and direction.

Building Community Life:

The Parish Life Coordinator would:

• personally foster community through pastoral availability, witness and presence;

• wherever possible, live within the community also as a witness;

• see that appropriate people and committees and resources are provided to build community and to provide opportunities and events when parishioners can come together to get to know one another;

• see that people are welcomed to the parish;

• strive to build a spirit of community within the parish.

Outreach and Service:

The Parish Life Coordinator would be responsible for:

• seeing that assistance is given to the poor and the needy and the homeless by establishing structures and committees to deal with emergency services;

• seeing that the parish community is encouraged to participate in outreach to others and is sensitive to social justice issues by ongoing social justice education on all parish levels, not an adjunct but a Gospel based charge and trust;

• arranging for and/or providing appropriate counseling and crisis intervention services;

• assisting or arranging for assistance to those seeking canonical advice and services from the Archdiocesan Tribunal.

Administration:

The Parish Life Coordinator would be responsible for:

• clear understanding of canonical requirements of administration and represent parish in their juridic affairs;

• hiring and supervising of parish staff;

• administering the financial aspects of the parish or supervising the staff person who is responsible for this area, i.e. bills, reports, records, collections;

• coordination of the annual planning/budgeting process;

• understanding of and commitment to Archdiocesan policies;

- working with the parish council and finance committee, seeing that stewardship is properly carried out;

- making sure that parish facilities and buildings are properly maintained and cared for;

- holding regular staff meetings;

- effective communication and collaboration among staff and council and committees;

- arranging parish schedules and providing for weekly bulletin;

- providing for facilitation of all parish activities and programs;

- provide for sacramental and other legal record keeping;

- relate where appropriate with parish or cluster school board.

Archdiocesan Involvement:

The Parish Life Coordinator would be responsible for:

- membership in area Ministeriums and cooperation with neighboring churches in providing services and programs as needed and appropriate;

- participation in the Regional Council;

- participation in other Archdiocesan and regional activities;

- attendance at Regional/Vicariate/Archdiocesan meetings of pastors.

V.
Envisioning the Future

A. Imagining What Can Be

After loss has been acknowledged and articulated in a parish community, there is gradual movement toward creating what will be new. The first sign of this is the group's focusing its energies on solving immediate problems as indicated in the previous chapter. The second sign that positive forces are beginning to surface is the desire to begin designing the immediate future. The creation of the new future is deeply rooted both in our imagination and in our tradition. In tapping our roots, we can create the future. Before we begin to use our logical and rational abilities to design what our parish will look like, we need to use our imaginations. The genius, Albert Einstein, is said to have discovered the theory of relativity in his imagination before he ever captured it in a logical framework.

59

Exercise 1

Spend some reflective time exploring the vision and dreams which are inside you using *one* of the designs suggested below.

    a.   Magic Hot Air Balloon

In a year or two from now you have a ride in a magic hot air balloon. The balloon is magic because it can pick up conversations on earth and has a telescopic lens which focuses on small groups of people engaged in their every day activities. It is also magic because it can stay up for long periods of time.

Choose to reflect on the questions below appropriate to your situation. Quiet yourself, close your eyes and reflect on the questions. Don't write answers at this time. Just allow your imagination to "walk around" the questions and focus where it chooses.

A year or two from now as you gently fly over your parish and the neighboring parishes, what activities do you see happening?

What buildings are being used?

What's happening in the buildings?

What are the children doing?

What are the older adults doing?

What are parents doing?

Who are the people in the parish?

If you asked someone to tell you about the greatest strength of the parish or parishes or school, what would they say?

What are the concerns you hear people discussing?

What's the most exciting thing you see happening or being discussed?

What is the parish life coordinator doing?

Who are the other parish leaders?

What other interesting things are you noticing in the parish? How do you feel about what you see?

After you have let your imagination reflect on these questions, jot down some of your imaginative memories!

b.   Wandering Minstrels

Imagine in a year or two you are wandering minstrels who meander into town and win the hearts of young and old alike. People invite you to their homes, their church(es), their community events. You learn much about the community. Quiet yourself and use your imagination to explore the following questions. Do not write at this time.

You learn that the major activities of the group include...

The major concerns of the parish council are...

The problems young people are coping with include...

The kind of music they appreciate most from you is...

The major events happen in these places...

The size of the parish or school is about...

The most exciting thing you learn is...

The parish life coordinator lives... and spends a good deal of time...

The other parish leaders include those who...

How do you feel about what you see?

Jot down the key points in this imaginative exercise.

As you share your images, what common elements emerge?

B. Pulling Our Dreams Together

In all our dreams there are probably some common elements.

In fact, the essential elements of what it means to be a church community are usually inherent in our imaginative visions. Return to your earlier reflections. In your visioning did you come up with aspects of community? Our tradition tells us that community is at the heart of what it means to be a parish. It can be found in many aspects of parish life. Sometimes community is seen in small groups of people meeting in homes to pray, study scriptures and promote justice. At other times it is seen in having coffee and donuts after liturgy or providing child care for all adult gatherings. Community support for grieving people, for those suffering marital separation, for the sick and elderly are but examples of what some aspects of community may mean.

Community is a basic tenant of Christian life. It's the foundation which suggests that God calls us as a people not just as individuals. It says we must be concerned about our neighbor and do what we can to create a better world for and with one another. The recent emphasis on being the people of God or the earlier image of the fifties, "body of Christ" reiterates our oldest communal tradition and diminishes a "Jesus and Me" spirituality.

Building community is not always easy because it goes against American individualism. On the other hand, if the parish church is to continue, the rediscovery and experience of community is essential. The loneliness and high degree of mobility of many Americans contributes to a felt need for community. People yearn to know that they are not in this world alone, that others experience what they do, that life is worth living and that the Christian message is one of hope and support.

Exercise 2

a. Reexamine your "In one or two years from now" reflections. List all aspects of community you found in your vision.

1.

2.

3.

4.

5.

b.   As you think about it now, are there other
community aspects you would like to see happening
within the next year?

List these:

C. Remembering God's Presence

Recalling God's presence is vital to the survival of the
parish community. Through prayer and worship the community remembers its identity as God's people and responds
with faith-filled hope to God's continual care. When the community gathers to pray and worship, its bondedness is con-
tinually solidified. It comes to worship as a community, and
it leaves as a more closely bonded community. The group assembled becomes the body of Christ, encounters God's word,
shares a meal with the presence of Jesus in the form of living
bread and wine and leaves with a mandate to love and serve
the Lord.

The power of God's word helps form the community. As
people listen to the Scriptures they identify with the struggles
and dreams of those who have gone before them. They see,
for instance, that the change which they are enduring is not
unlike Abraham's call to leave all that was home and begin
anew. Perhaps they recognize something of themselves in
the call of Miriam to lead the people singing and dancing to

the new life which lay beyond their familiar life in Egypt. In responding to God's word, people are rooted in the past, enlightened in the present and strengthened to move to the future.

Communal prayer may be experienced in small groups that meet in homes to pray and study scripture as well as in the large assembly which gathers on Sunday. In fact, in some cases as a result of the Eucharist not being available on a daily basis in parishes, small groups whose prayer stems from the liturgy of the word are forming. These groups provide good experiences of community as well as prayer and outreach activities.

Exercise 3

a. Reflect on your earlier imaginative visioning.
What elements of prayer and worship were present?

b. As you think of it now, do you wish to add any others?

D. Reaching Out

A third vital element in parish life is outreach. A parish is called not just to look inward, but to provide service to its own members as well as to the larger community. Parishes are challenged to follow the experience of the early Christian communities. The Acts of the Apostles reflects a community concerned about the poor, the widows and orphans. It points to the invitation to share material goods so all will have what is needed.

Today we are called to provide many of the same things but also to look beyond our immediate community to create a more just society. This may mean looking at environmental issues at home and abroad, racial issues and gender in the United States as well as in the world, educational, economic and peace concerns.

The social justice or outreach dimension is not optional to parish life. It is an integral part of the Gospel. Admittedly, a parish may choose certain issues to deal with and ignore others because it doesn't have resources to be involved in too many things. The important point is that the service dimension of the Gospel must be a visible element in parish life.

Exercise 4

a.   Reexamine your parish vision. What elements of social justice do you find there?

b.   Do you wish to add others? If so, describe these.

Exercise 5

Reflect on your visions and discussions and list the common elements you wish to have incorporated in your parish in the future.

Exercise 6

If your parish will have a parish life coordinator, what roles would you expect the person to play in relation to building community, leading prayer and promoting social justice?

Prayer And Ritual

Gathering Song "City of God" (verse 1 and refrain) by Dan Schutte, or other appropriate song

Call To Prayer

Leader: God of the universe you have given us signs of new life amidst our experience of great loss. Encourage us to nurture the hopeful signs as we begin to envision our future. We ask this in the name of Jesus, our Lord.

All: AMEN.

Reading   Colossians 3:12-17 (adapted)

You are God's chosen race, God's saints; God loves you, and you should be clothed in sincere compassion, in kindness and humility, gentleness and patience. Bear with one another; forgive each other as soon as a quarrel begins. The Lord has forgiven you; now you must do the same. Over all these clothes, to keep them together and complete them, put on love. And may the peace of Christ reign in your hearts, because it is for this that you were called together as parts of one body. Always be thankful.

Let the message of Christ, in all its richness, find a home with you. Teach each other, and advise each other, in all wisdom. With gratitude in your hearts sing psalms and hymns and inspired songs to God, and never say or do anything except in the name of the Lord Jesus, giving thanks to God through him.

Reflection

Response   Isaiah 12 (adapted)

Right: I give thanks to you, Yahweh,
you were angry with me but your anger
is appeased and you have given me
consolation.

Left: See now, God is my salvation
I have trust now and no fear,
for Yahweh is my strength, my song,
my salvation.

Right: And you will draw water joyfully
from the springs of salvation.
That day, you will say:
Give thanks to Yahweh,
call God's name aloud.

Left: Proclaim God's deeds to the people,
declare God's name sublime.

Right: Sing of Yahweh, for God has done
           marvelous things,
           let them be made known to the whole world.

Left: Cry out for joy and gladness,
           you dwellers in Zion,
           for great in the midst of you
           is the Holy One of Israel.

Ritualizing Our Visions

Recall the most exciting or challenging part of your vision for the future. Be prepared to share it in the format listed below.

Leader: God, through your gifts we have been able
           to begin to envision our future. We ask you
           to strengthen us to fulfill our dreams of
           making your presence better known on earth.
           We ask this in the name of Jesus, the Lord.

All: AMEN.

Leader: Anointing is a sign of being strengthened.
           Athletes were anointed before beginning
           races, soldiers before going to battle. This
           day we are anointed to be strengthened to
           work toward fulfilling our dreams of fulfilling
           God's reign on earth.

Individuals come forward requesting to be anointed by saying:

           "Anoint me in the name of Jesus to _____"
           (Name part of your vision, or say, "continue
           to build up the body of Christ".)

If the Parish Life Coordinator or other designated leader (pastor, principal, etc.) are present have them come forward first.

Leader: I anoint you with the sign of the cross, in the name of the Father, Son and Holy Spirit to continue your efforts for (Name) Parish.

Closing Song   "City of God," by Dan Schutte, or other appropriate song

VI.

Creating a Ministering Community

Often at times of great change there is the opportunity to reevaluate and become more of what we want to be. All of what we have been emerges as fodder for what we will become. Our stories, our losses, our dreams are interwoven into the fabric of the future we are creating.

When basic assumptions, such as having a resident pastor or being a mission of a parish which has one, are uprooted, people are often forced to ask the basic questions. What's the purpose of the parish? Why do we exist? Where are we going? What does it mean to be Church? What steps do we take to become more of what we wish to be?

One appropriate image for a contemporary parish is that of ministering community. Ministry is a word used extensively in the Church today. This is seen partly as a result of the declining numbers of vocations to the ordained priesthood and religious life and partly because there is a new awareness that the call to minister is inherent in Baptism. The need for the laity to be more involved in the Church community is becoming increasingly evident.

A framework which can be helpful in understanding ministry and who we are called to be as laity is the American Bishops' Pastoral, *Called and Gifted: The American Catholic Laity.* The bishops wrote this to commemorate the fifteenth anniversary of the issuance of the Vatican II document, "The Decree on the Apostolate of the Laity." The Bishops' Pastoral calls the laity to four things: adulthood, holiness, ministry and community. In examining these challenges, we can cull insights about what we need to do to continue creating a ministering parish community.

A. Call to Adulthood

The bishops state:

> "One of the chief characteristics of lay men and women today is their growing sense of being adult members of the Church. Adulthood implies knowledge, experience and awareness, freedom and responsibility and mutuality in relationships."

In this document, the bishops recognize the maturity of adults and their interdependence with the Church. In other words, in this pastoral there is a sense of mutuality and respect which may not have been as explicit in the past. To glean further insights into the significance of the call to adulthood, use the following exercise.

Exercise 1

a. Think of children. What are some of their primary characteristics?

   1.

   2.

   3.

   4.

   5.

b. In contrast what are some of the primary characteristics of adults?

   1.

   2.

   3.

   4.

   5.

c. What is the significance of what adults bring to the Church?

d. Name times when you feel like your knowledge, experience, awareness, freedom and responsibility have been valued by the Church.

   Knowledge_____

   Experience _____

Awareness_____

Freedom _____

Responsibility _____

How did you feel about this?

e. As you reflect on the call to adulthood in the Church, what image comes to mind? Draw it or describe it here. Is there an image which reflects the group perceptions of the call to adulthood?

f. In working through the transition process in your parish, name the ways you have been called to adulthood.

g. What's been challenging about the call?

h. What's been perplexing about the call?

B. Call to Holiness

Quoting from the Vatican II document on the Church, the bishops remind the laity:

> "Thus it is evident to everyone that all the faithful of Christ of whatever rank or status are called to the fullness of Christian life and to the perfections of charity. By this holiness a more human way of life is promoted even in this earthly society." (Lumen Gentian #40)

Before the Second Vatican Council the Church promoted the concept that priests and vowed religious were called to a greater degree of holiness than the laity. Since the council the universal call to holiness has been espoused. Terms like "spirituality of the laity" arose as a way to delineate the holiness which is found in everyday life.

The integration of holiness and life is related to a "more human way of life...in earthly society." The bishops describe the process of growing in holiness in the

> "very web of existence...in and through the events of the world, the pluralism of modern living, the complex decisions and conflicting values...the richness and fragility of sexual relationships, the delicate balance between activity and stillness, presence and privacy, love and loss."

The bishops articulate well the context of life for many people. They tell us that it is in this ambiguous and at times perplexing milieu that we discover and respond to God's presence. It is in this context that we grow in holiness.

Exercise 2

a. Describe the phrases which most excite you in the bishops' call to holiness. Why do you find these ideas exciting?

b. Choose three or four of the following phrases and recall one of your experiences related to the phrase.

Call to Holiness	My Experience
holiness as promoting a more human way of life	
holiness in the very web of existence	
holiness in and through world events	
holiness in the pluralism of modern living	
holiness in complex decisions	
holiness in conflicting values	
holiness in the richness and fragility of sexual relationships	

holiness in the
balance between activity
and stillness

holiness in
presence and privacy

holiness in love
and loss

c. The bishops state that the spiritual needs of lay
people must be met in the parish. Name ways your
parish is currently responding to these needs.

d. In what other ways might the parish meet the
needs of lay people striving for holiness?

e. What image comes to mind as you picture the
parish(es) serving the hunger for holiness found
among the laity?

f. What problems do you foresee in the area of
spirituality of the laity?

g. What steps need to be taken to help people see that spirituality is inherent in life?

h. What traditions does your community have which invite lay people to see their call to holiness?

i. Is there any need to strengthen these or change them? If so, how?

j. If your transition issue involves school, how do schools contribute to the call to holiness of the laity?

C. Call to Ministry

The Degree on the Apostolate of the Laity (#3) states that the laity has the right and duty to use their gifts for the "good of humankind and for the upbuilding of the Church." The bishops use St. Paul's image of the body to remind believers of their call to use their gifts for the good of others. The document calls the clergy to "call forth, identify, coordinate and affirm" the gifts of the laity—and to do this in such a way that promotes the "solidarity between laity and clergy."

Exercise 3

a.   Recall and name ways you have used your gifts
     for the good of humankind.

b.   How have your gifts made a difference in the
     lives of others?

c.   Recall and name some ways you have used your
     gifts for the building of the Church community.

d.   How have your gifts made a difference to the
     Church community?

e.   In the future what ways do you feel called to use
     your gifts for the good of people in general and/or
     the Church in particular?

f.   Which of your gifts do you feel are more effectively
     used in collaboration with others? Why?

g. As a group how do you feel the laity respond to the call to ministry? What encouragement do they receive? What obstacles do they face?

h. If you have a parish life coordinator how does the person reflect the call to holiness.

D. Call to Community

The bishops, citing the Vatican Council (Lumen Gentium #11), link the call to build community to family life. In calling the family the domestic Church, they point to the spirit of interdependence, intimacy, support, acceptance and availability found in families as viable elements which should be found in parish communities. Acknowledging that the family is a basic community the bishops urge parishes to both support the family and model themselves after the family. The bishops mention both intentional communities and basic Christian communities as signs of small group life modeled after families.

The insights gleaned from examining the call to adulthood, holiness, ministry and community as well as our previous reflections on community, prayer and worship and service provide a solid foundation to continue or begin to design the parishes for the twenty-first century. The Church of the next era will, according to current projections, have fewer ordained priests and more active lay participation working to help parishes become greater signs of ministering communities.

Exercise 4

a. What elements of family life do you feel are most appropriately transferred to parish life? Why?

b. Do you feel a sense of community is important for the survival of your parish(es)? If so, why?

c. What obstacles are there to creating community?

d. What positive thrusts are there for creating community?

e. What image comes to your mind as you think of the parish as a ministering community?

f. What are some steps you feel need to be taken to create or recreate your parish into a ministering community?

g.   What elements in its history support this thrust?

Prayer And Ritual

Gathering Song "Here I Am Lord" (verse 1 and refrain) by
Dan Schutte or another appropriate song

Call To Prayer

Leader: God, you have called us to be your priestly
people. Strengthen us as we continue to be
your people and create communities which
minister to others. We ask this in the
name of Jesus.

All: AMEN.

Reading   Hebrews 13:1-8

Continue to love each other like brothers
and sisters, and remember always to welcome
strangers, for by doing this, some people
have entertained angels without knowing it.
Keep in mind those who are in prison, as
though you were in prison with them; and
those who are being badly treated, since you
too are in the one body. Marriage is to be
honoured by all, and marriages are to be
kept undefiled, because fornicators and
adulterers will come under God's judgement.
Put greed out of your lives and be content
with whatever you have; God has said: I will
not fail you or desert you, and so we can

say with confidence: With the Lord to help me,
I fear nothing: what can people do to me?

Remember your leaders, who preached the word
of God to you, and as you reflect on the
outcome of their lives, imitate their faith.

Silent Reflection

Response   Psalm 85 (adapted)

Men: Yahweh you favour your own country,
you bring back the captives of Jacob,
you take your people's guilt away,
you blot out all their sins,
you retract all your anger,
you abjure your fiery rage.

Women: For those who fear God's saving help is near
and the glory will live in our country.

All: Righteousness will always precede
the Lord,
Peace will follow God's footsteps.

Ritualizing Our Gifts

Reflection   What gifts do I bring to the community?
To which of the following categories do
your gifts belong:
1) administration,
2) teaching or catechizing,
3) visiting sick or shut-ins,
4) contributing to prayer and worship,
5) helping the poor,
6) maintaining the grounds,
7) feeding the hungry, or
8) other.

Leader: (As the leader(s) call for people with
gifts in the above categories, go forward to
share your gift and be commissioned to use
it for the world and the community.)

Each of us received the gifts of the spirit at
Baptism. As we have grown in Christian
maturity we have discovered our gifts and
have and/or will use them for the good
of the community.

Will those who have gifts in administration
come forward.

(People come forward.)

What gifts do you bring?

Individuals: I bring the gift of _____.

Leader: (*Laying hands on head*) I commission you to
use your gift for the good of the world
and this community.

Repeat this process for each category.

Closing Song "Here I Am Lord" (verses 2 and 3 and refrain),
by Dan Schutte, or other appropriate song